SCHOLASTIC

TEACHING STRUGGLING READERS TO TACKLE MATH WORD PROBLEMS

by Audrey Trapolsi

New York ○ Toronto ○ London ○ Auckland ○ Sydney
New Delhi ○ Mexico City ○ Hong Kong ○ Buenos Aires

Teaching *Resources*

Dedication
For my teachers

Editors: Jack Silbert, Maria L. Chang
Cover design: Jorge J. Namerow
Interior design: Grafica Inc.
Illustrator: Mike Moran

ISBN: 978-0-545-20717-1

6 7 8 9 10   40   19 18 17 16

Contents

Introduction

Most word-problem math instruction focuses on teaching a range of strategies—such as Guess and Check, Draw a Picture, Make an Organized List, and so on—to solve problems, and then helping students select the most appropriate strategy for a particular problem.

That brand of word-problem instruction works well for some students. Struggling readers, meanwhile, can't even begin to approach the math in a word problem because they misunderstand the problem at the language level. If a student does not understand what's going on in a word problem, how can he or she hope to successfully tackle the actual math?

That's where this book comes in. *Teaching Struggling Readers to Tackle Math Word Problems* will reach those struggling readers (at a 2nd- to 3rd-grade level) who continue to be frustrated by word problems. In this book, we examine the word-problem structure much more closely than most math books do and work directly with specific math language that holds important cues for problem solving. The lessons and activities reinforce strategies such as visualizing, predicting, reflecting about reading, and other skills typically learned in language arts, to help every learner untangle word problems and approach problem solving with new confidence.

WHAT'S INSIDE

This book features several strategy lessons in which students learn to dissect word problems and identify key words and phrases, as well as activities and situations that signal what type of math operation a problem calls for. Recognizing different types of word problems will help strengthen students' words-to-numbers connection. Understanding the "math story"—where to start reading, what cue words to look out for, what the problem describes, and how to stay focused when there are multiple steps—will help readers solve problems correctly.

Reproducible practice pages that follow each strategy lesson scaffold students from guided practice to independent performance, helping reinforce their understanding in a variety of ways—through cloze practice, problem-equation matching, highlighting important information, rearranging scrambled sentences, and more. Some of the activities do not involve writing or numbers, but they do involve the math-story thinking. Visual organizers help students analyze word problems, just as they can help struggling readers understand the books they read.

Another key component to understanding word problems is actually creating your own. Students will have several opportunities to write their own word problems and share them with classmates. By encouraging children to be math writers, we help them approach math in a new way and bring new thinking to word problems. Practice as math writers will help students grow as math readers.

The latter part of the book offers several games and activities that further reinforce learning. There are opportunities for whole-class learning, collaborative work with small groups and partners, or independent practice.

Regardless of format, all the activities are designed to help students make a connection between words and numbers and to use many of the same strategies they are learning in reading class—visualization, prediction, and self-monitoring—to unlock the puzzle of word problems.

Meeting the Common Core State Standards

The lessons and activities in this book meet the following standards in mathematics and reading:

MATHEMATICS STANDARDS

GRADE 2
2.OA Operations and Algebraic Thinking
- Represent and solve problems involving addition and subtraction.
- Work with equal groups of objects to gain foundations for multiplication.

GRADE 3
3.OA Operations and Algebraic Thinking
- Represent and solve problems involving multiplication and division.
- Understand properties of multiplication and the relationship between multiplication and division.
- Multiply and divide within 100.
- Solve problems involving the four operations, and identify and explain patterns in arithmetic.

3.NF Number and Operations—Fractions
- Develop understanding of fractions as numbers.

GRADE 4
4.OA Operations and Algebraic Thinking
- Use the four operations with whole numbers to solve problems.

GRADE 5
5.OA Operations and Algebraic Thinking
- Write and interpret numerical expressions.

READING STANDARDS FOR INFORMATIONAL TEXT

GRADE 3
RI.3.1 Ask and answer questions to demonstrate understanding of a text, referring explicitly to the text as the basis for the answers.

RI.3.2 Determine the main idea of a text; recount the key details and explain how they support the main idea.

RI.3.4 Determine the meaning of general academic and domain-specific words and phrases in a text relevant to a grade topic or subject area.

RI.3.7 Use information gained from illustrations and the words in a text to demonstrate understanding of the text.

RI.3.8 Describe the logical connection between particular sentences and paragraphs in a text.

GRADE 4
RI.4.1 Refer to details and examples in a text when explaining what the text says explicitly and when drawing inferences from the text.

RI.4.2 Determine the main idea of a text and explain how it is supported by key details; summarize the text.

RI.4.4 Determine the meaning of general academic and domain-specific words and phrases in a text relevant to a grade topic or subject area.

RI.4.7 Interpret information presented visually, orally, or quantitatively and explain how the information contributes to an understanding of the text in which it appears.

GRADE 5
RI.5.1 Quote accurately from a text when explaining what the text says explicitly and when drawing inferences from the text.

RI.5.3 Explain the relationships or interactions between two or more events, ideas, or concepts in a technical text based on specific information in the text.

RI.5.4 Determine the meaning of general academic and domain-specific words and phrases in a text relevant to a grade topic or subject area.

Source: Common Core State Standards Initiative http://www.corestandards.org/the-standards

STRATEGY LESSON

Reading and Understanding Addition Problems

TEACHER TALK

Ask students: *Mathematicians, what do you already know about addition word problems? What happens in addition story problems?* Possible answers include:

- Numbers get bigger.
- You get more stuff.
- You have stuff and then add stuff to what you already have.
- Somebody gives somebody something.

READ AND DISCUSS

Distribute copies of Understanding Addition Problems (page 7) to students. If possible, display a copy on the overhead or interactive whiteboard.

Tell students: *Here are four word problems. Two of these problems use addition.* Read the problems aloud. Ask: *Which problems do you think use addition? How do you know?* Pair up students and have them talk to each other about their ideas. After students have shared with their partners, invite volunteers to share their thinking with the whole class. (Students should recognize that questions 1 and 4 are the addition problems.) Record their ideas on the whiteboard or on chart paper.

Discuss strategies that some students may already be using, such as:

- identify words and phrases that signal addition; for example, *all together, in all, total, more*
- identify activities or situations that involve addition; for example, counting objects, finding an amount, combining numbers, amounts getting bigger

Reinforce these strategies by having students continue their guided practice. Photocopy the following reproducibles for students and have them work on the pages over the next few days. Be sure to discuss their answers, reinforcing addition vocabulary and concepts.

- Addition Draw-It (page 8)
- Addition Fill-in (page 9)
- Addition Pick-the-Question (page 10)

EXTEND THEIR THINKING

Refer back to the Understanding Addition Problems reproducible. Ask students: *What type of problem are questions 2 and 3? How do you know?* (Question 2 is a subtraction problem, and question 3 is a division problem.)

Understanding Addition Problems

Which two of these word problems are about addition? Circle the addition problems. Also circle the clue words in those problems that signal addition. Then solve the problems.

1. Sanjana collects wild animal trading cards. She has 37 jungle animal cards. She gets 48 more cards for her birthday. How many cards does she have all together?

2. Victor has 86 purple jelly beans. He shares with his brother James and gives him 28 jelly beans. How many does Victor have left?

3. Pamela has 20 sparkle bracelets. She puts them in groups of four bracelets. How many groups of bracelets does she have?

4. Yuri has 50 cents. He finds three dimes on the playground and a nickel in his jacket pocket. How much money does he have now?

Addition Draw-It

We can use pictures to represent a word problem. Let's take a look at this problem:

Shavonne has 2 balloons. Her brother brings her 3 more balloons. How many does Shavonne have in all?

We can draw this picture:

We can also write it as a math problem: 2 + 3 = 5

....

Now draw a picture for this problem:

Luis has 3 balloons. He buys one more balloon. How many balloons does he have in all?

Now write it as a math problem, with numbers. Solve.

....

On the back of the paper, draw a picture for this problem, and then write it as a math problem with numbers. Solve.

Clara has 8 smiley-face stickers. Her mom gives her 7 more smiley-face stickers. How many does Clara have in all?

Teaching Struggling Readers to Tackle Math Word Problems © 2012 by Audrey Trapolsi, Scholastic Teaching Resources

Addition Fill-in

Use the word bank to fill in each blank with the correct word or number.
Then solve the problems.

1. Colleen and Rayna played a math card game. Colleen scored 65 points

in game one and 125 _____ in game two. Rayna _____

75 points in _____ one and 115 points in game two.

How _____ points did they score _____ together?

WORD BANK
points
scored
many
all
game

2. Jamal was buying ingredients to make _____ salad. He

_____ two pineapples, one _____, three bananas,

and _____ oranges. _____ many fruits

_____ he buy _____ all?

fruit
How
watermelon
six
bought
did
in

3. Kizzy brought cupcakes to school for her birthday. She brought

12 chocolate _____, 8 _____ cupcakes, and

_____ strawberry cupcakes. How many cupcakes did

she _____ all _____?

together
cupcakes
vanilla
4
bring

4. Alexander _____ comic books. He has 28 Wolfman

comic books, _____ Dracula comic _____, and

11 Frankenstein _____ books. How many comic books

_____ he _____ in all?

does
have
comic
19
collects
books

Addition Pick-the-Question

Circle the correct question to finish each word problem. Solve.

1. Hanna goes on a class trip to the zoo. She sees 4 lions,
   6 tigers, 5 flamingos, and 12 camels.

   a. How many more animals does Hanna have?

   b. How many animals does she see in all?

   c. How many more animals are at the zoo?

   d. How long was Hanna at the zoo?

2. Every Saturday, Thomas gets $6 for his allowance. There are 4 Saturdays in the
   month of August.

   a. How much does Thomas get for his birthday?

   b. How many days is Thomas's vacation?

   c. How much money does Thomas get in August?

   d. How many weeks will it take Thomas to save for a bicycle?

3. The Jackson Jaguars Little League team scored 2 runs in the first inning, 3 runs in
   the fourth inning, and then 1 run in the sixth inning.

   a. Did they Jaguars win the game?

   b. What time was the game over?

   c. Who scored the winning run?

   d. How many runs did they score in all?

4. Kyla rides her scooter for 1 hour on Monday, 2 hours on Tuesday, and 4 hours
   on Wednesday.

   a. What time does Kyla come home?

   b. How many hours does Kyla ride in all?

   c. How far is it to school?

   d. How many hours does Robin ride her scooter?

5. Keith is playing the Spiders From Outer Space video game. He scores 9,500 points
   on level one. He scores 12,000 points on level two.

   a. How many points does Keith score in all?

   b. How many points will he score on level three?

   c. How many more points does Jonathan score?

   d. How many points does it take to win the game?

Teaching Struggling Readers to Tackle Math Word Problems © 2012 by Audrey Trapolsi, Scholastic Teaching Resources

Reading and Understanding Multiplication Problems

TEACHER TALK

Tell students: *Mathematicians, now that you have shown what you know about reading addition problems, we're going to look at multiplication problems and what kind of reading you can expect to find in these word problems.* Ask: *What happens in multiplication story problems?* Possible answers include:

- ◆ Numbers get bigger.
- ◆ You have groups of things.
- ◆ You put things in rows.
- ◆ You use the word *times* or *groups*.

READ AND DISCUSS

Distribute copies of Understanding Multiplication Problems (page 12) to students. If possible, display a copy on the overhead or interactive whiteboard.

Tell students: *Here are six word problems. Two of these problems use multiplication.* Read the problems aloud. Ask: *Which problems do you think use multiplication? How do you know?* Pair up students and have them talk to each other about their ideas. After students have shared with their partners, invite volunteers to share their thinking with the whole class. (Students should recognize that questions 3 and 5 are the multiplication problems.) Record their ideas on the whiteboard or on chart paper.

Discuss strategies that some students may already be using, such as:

- ◆ identify words and phrases that signal multiplication; for example, *all together, each, times, groups, in all, total, more*
- ◆ identify activities or situations that involve multiplication; for example, putting things in rows, groups, or containers; or amounts getting bigger

Guide students to notice that some of the words and activities that signal multiplication are similar to those that relate to addition. Remind them that multiplication is repeated addition; for example, 3 x 4 is the same as 3 + 3 + 3 + 3.

Reinforce these strategies by having students continue their guided practice. Photocopy the following reproducibles for students and have them work on the pages over the next few days. Be sure to discuss their answers, reinforcing multiplication vocabulary and concepts.

- ◆ Visual Organizer: Comparing Addition and Multiplication (page 13)
- ◆ Multiplication Fill-In (page 14)

EXTEND THEIR THINKING

Refer back to the Understanding Multiplication Problems reproducible. Ask students: *What type of problem are questions 1, 2, 4, and 6? How do you know?* (Questions 1 and 6 are subtraction problems, and questions 2 and 4 are division problems.)

Understanding Multiplication Problems

Which two of these word problems are about multiplication? Circle the multiplication problems. Also circle the clue words in those problems that signal multiplication. Then solve the problems.

1. There are 238 students in the fourth grade at Shady Glen Elementary School. There are 327 students in the fifth grade. How many more fifth graders are there?

2. Mario played street hockey for 30 minutes on Monday, 45 minutes on Wednesday, and 60 minutes on Saturday. What was his average playing time for the three days?

3. Ina bought 4 bags of pretzels for $0.89 each. How much did she spend in all?

4. Phillipa paid $12.80 for 4 pairs of scissors. How much was each pair of scissors?

5. Mrs. Epstein's class made clay animals for a zoo project. Each animal used 6 ounces of clay. There are 20 students in Mrs. Epstein's class. How many ounces of clay did they use all together?

6. Ursula tied a 60-foot-long string to her kite. Fernando tied a 30-yard-long string to his kite. Whose string was longer?

Teaching Struggling Readers to Tackle Math Word Problems © 2012 by Audrey Trapolsi, Scholastic Teaching Resources

Visual Organizer: Comparing Addition and Multiplication

In the top ring, write words and ideas that you know about addition. In the bottom ring, write words and ideas that you know about multiplication. Fill in the overlapping space with words and ideas that are true for both addition and multiplication.

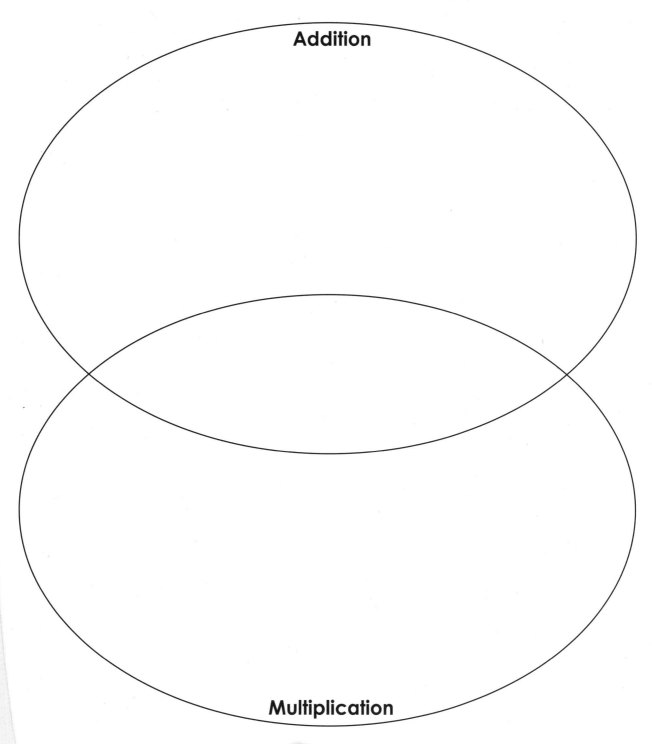

Addition

Multiplication

Name: _____

Multiplication Fill-in

Use the word bank to fill in each blank with the correct word or number.
Then solve the problems.

1. Yuri wants to make _____ paper

airplanes for _____ boy in his

_____. There are 13 boys in Yuri's

class. How many _____ does Yuri

need to _____ in _____?

....

2. The Fish Headquarters _____ shop has 5 _____

as many goldfish _____ guppies. They have _____

guppies. How many goldfish do they _____?

....

3. Frances bought 6 _____ of gumballs. Each pound of

gumballs _____ $4.50. How _____ did

Frances _____ in all?

....

4. Henry packed 4 sleeping _____ in his backpack for

his _____ trip. _____ sleeping bag

weighs 6 pounds. _____ much do all the sleeping bags

_____ together?

Teaching Struggling Readers to Tackle Math Word Problems © 2012 by Audrey Trapolsi, Scholastic Teaching Resources

STRATEGY LESSON

Reading and Understanding Subtraction Problems

TEACHER TALK

Tell students: *Mathematicians, you know a lot about reading word problems that use addition and multiplication. Today we're going to look at what happens in word problems that use subtraction.* Ask: *What happens in subtraction story problems? What kinds of situations do you see in those problems?* Possible answers include:

- ◆ Numbers get smaller.
- ◆ You give things away.
- ◆ You spend money.
- ◆ You have money or stuff that's left.

READ AND DISCUSS

Distribute copies of Understanding Subtraction Problems (page 16). If possible, display a copy on the overhead or interactive whiteboard.

Tell students: *Here are four word problems. Two of these word problems use subtraction.* Read the problems aloud. Ask: *Which problems do you think use subtraction? How do you know?* Pair up students and have them talk to each other about their ideas. After students have shared with their partners, invite volunteers to share their thinking with the whole class. (Students should recognize that questions 2 and 3 are subtraction problems.) Record their ideas on the whiteboard or on chart paper.

Discuss strategies that some students may already be using, such as:

- ◆ identify words and phrases that signal subtraction, such as: *left, how many more, how much more, change*
- ◆ identify comparison words that signal subtraction, such as *longer* or *farther*
- ◆ identify activities or situations that involve subtraction, such as receiving change, comparing amounts, giving away or using up items

Reinforce these strategies by having students continue their guided practice. Photocopy the following reproducibles for students and have them work on the pages over the next few days. Be sure to discuss their answers, reinforcing subtraction vocabulary and concepts.

- ◆ Subtraction Pick-the-Question (page 17)
- ◆ Subtraction Fill-In (page 18)
- ◆ Equation Matching (page 19)

EXTEND THEIR THINKING

Refer back to the Understanding Subtraction Problems reproducible. Ask students: *What type of problem are questions 1 and 4? How do you know?* (Questions 1 and 4 are addition problems.)

Understanding Subtraction Problems

Which two of these word problems are about subtraction? Circle the subtraction problems. Also circle the clue words in those problems that signal subtraction. Then solve the problems.

1. Joyce saved $16.50 to spend at the book fair. Her mom gave her $5.00 more. How much did she have all together?

2. Kieran had 145 comic books. He gave 28 to his best friend. How many comic books does Kieran have left?

3. Lara's parents drive her 37 miles to summer camp. Jill's parents drive her 18 miles to summer camp. How much farther is Lara's drive?

4. Will spent 45 minutes at the library, 2 hours at the Robot Club, and 90 minutes at his best friend's house. How much time did Will spend outside his home in total?

Teaching Struggling Readers to Tackle Math Word Problems © 2012 by Audrey Trapolsi, Scholastic Teaching Resources

Name: _____

Subtraction Pick-the-Question

For each word problem, choose the math question that would fit best to make a subtraction problem. Solve.

1. There are 284 girls in the fifth grade at Plum Valley Elementary. There are 260 boys in the fifth grade.

    a. How many fifth graders are there in all?

    b. How many more girls are there than boys?

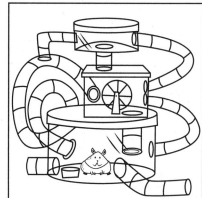

2. Hector has 18 feet of plastic tunnels for his Hamster Palace set. Indira has 14 feet of tunnels for her set.

    a. How many more feet of tunnels does Hector have than Indira?

    b. How many feet of tunnel do they have all together?

3. Shawnee can stand on one leg for 135 seconds. Shawnee's mom can stand on one leg for 90 seconds.

    a. What is the average time they can stand on one leg?

    b. How much longer can Shawnee stand on one leg than her mom?

4. In 30 seconds, Tami can run 80 feet. Jalissa can run 85 feet.

    a. How far can they both run in a minute?

    b. How much farther can Jalissa run than Tami?

5. For his special Island Fruit Party punch, Javier uses 24 ounces of pineapple juice and 18 ounces of apple juice.

    a. How much fruit juice does Javier use all together?

    b. How much more pineapple juice does he use than apple juice?

6. Ira can throw a baseball 20 yards and 2 feet. Owen can throw a baseball 19 yards and 1 foot.

    a. How much farther can Ira throw a baseball than Owen?

    b. How many balls can Ira throw in an hour?

Name: _____

Subtraction Fill-in

Use the word bank to fill in each blank with the correct word or number. Then solve the problems.

1. Eli made a paper _____ chain that is 462 paper clips _____.

Ellen _____ 521 _____ clips to make her chain. _____

many _____ paper clips did Ellen _____?

2. There are 833 players in the _____ Soccer League. 478 _____ the

players are _____. How _____ of the _____ are girls?

3. Flying Danger Squad players must score 25,000 _____ to

_____ to _____ two. Zoe has scored 17,500 points.

How many _____ points does she need to _____ before

_____ can advance to level _____?

4. It is 4,124 _____ from Woodsville to _____. _____

is 3,988 miles from Woodsville _____ Stumpton. How much

_____ is it to Leaftown _____ to Stumpton?

5. Petra _____ 98 Glow-Pony _____. She gave 17 to

Amanda and _____ to Jenna. How _____ stickers does

_____ have _____?

6. Kenji's cat Cheddar weighs 14 _____. His _____

Feta _____ 12 pounds, _____ ounces. How much

_____ does Cheddar _____?

Equation Matching

Circle the letter of the equation that matches each word problem. Solve.

1. Adam bought a desk hockey set for $18.75. He gave $20.00 to the salesperson. How much change did he receive?

    a. $18.75 – $1.25 = ?

    b. $20.00 – $18.75 = ?

    c. $18.75 + $20.00 = ?

    d. None of these

2. Regular chocolate cupcakes cost $12.50 for 6 cupcakes. Super-Deluxe chocolate cupcakes cost $16.00 for 6 cupcakes. How much more do the 6 Super-Deluxe cupcakes cost?

    a. $16.00 – $12.50 = ?

    b. $16.00 + $12.50 = ?

    c. $20.00 – $16.00 = ?

    d. $20.00 – $12.50 =?

3. By the end of the Zoo Festival, Kendra had spent $11.40 and Edward had spent $14.00. How much more did Edward spend than Kendra?

    a. $20.00 – $14.00 = ?

    b. $14.00 + $11.40 = ?

    c. $20.00 – $11.40 = ?

    d. $14.00 – $11.40 = ?

4. Jared and Byron played Alien Revenge on Jared's Gameplosion system. Jared got 19,500 points and Byron got 32,000 points. How many more points did Byron get?

    a. 41,500 – 32,000 = ?

    b. 19,500 – 32,000 = ?

    c. 32,000 + 19,500 = ?

    d. 32,000 – 19,500 = ?

Reading and Understanding Division Problems

TEACHER TALK

Tell students: *Mathematicians, you now know a lot about reading word problems that use addition, subtraction, and multiplication. Today we're going to look at what happens in word problems that use division.* Ask: *What happens in division story problems? What kinds of situations do you see in those problems?* Possible answers include:

- ◆ You share stuff evenly or fairly.
- ◆ You take a big group of things and put them into smaller groups that are equal.
- ◆ You know how much money you spent on several things and you need to find out how much each thing costs (unit price).

READ AND DISCUSS

Distribute copies of Understanding Division Problems (page 21) to students. If possible, display a copy on the overhead or interactive whiteboard.

Tell students: *Here are four word problems. Two of these word problems use division.* Read the problems aloud. Ask: *Which problems do you think use division? How do you know?* Pair up students and have them discuss their ideas with each other. After students have shared with their partners, invite volunteers to share their thinking with the whole class. (Students should recognize that questions 1 and 4 are the division problems.) Record their ideas on the whiteboard or on chart paper. Ask: *How are division problems similar to multiplication problems?* (They both involve putting things in groups.) *How are they different?* (In division, you start with a large number and find out how it breaks down evenly into smaller groups. In multiplication, you combine groups of equal size to find out how many there are in all.)

Discuss strategies that some students may already be using, such as:

- ◆ identify clue words that can signal division; for example, *each, divided, split, equally*
- ◆ identify situations in which people share evenly and problems that involve groups in which you are given the total number of items you have.

Reinforce these strategies by having students continue their guided practice. Photocopy the following reproducibles for students and have them work on the pages over the next few days. Be sure to discuss their answers, reinforcing division vocabulary and concepts.

- ◆ Division Fill-In (page 22)
- ◆ Division Pick-the-Question (page 23)
- ◆ Understanding "Each" Problems (page 24)

EXTEND THEIR THINKING

Refer back to the Understanding Division Problems reproducible. Ask students: *What type of problem are questions 2 and 3? How do you know?* (Question 2 is a combination of multiplication and subtraction, and question 3 is a subtraction problem.)

Understanding Division Problems

Which two of these word problems are about division? Circle the division problems. Also circle the clue words in those problems that signal division. Then solve the problems.

1. Dinah earned $20 walking dogs last month.

She earns $4 for each dog she walks.

How many dogs did she walk last month?

2. Niall wants to buy 4 cartons of juice. Each carton cost $1.25. Niall has a $5.00 bill. Does he have enough money?

3. Bettina's book is 243 pages long. She has already read 92 pages. How many more pages does she have to read?

4. Quinn baked cookies for his party. He baked 30 cookies and has 6 friends at the party. Each friend will get the same number of cookies. How many cookies will each friend get?

Name: _____

Division Fill-in

Use the word bank to fill in each blank with the correct word or number.

1. Matteo can fit 7 _____ into _____ shoe box. He has _____

cars. How many _____ will he need for _____ of his cars?

2. There are _____ students in Mr. Mulligan's _____.

The _____ sit in _____ of _____. How

_____ students are in _____ row?

3. Roger _____ breakfast for his _____. He makes _____

pancakes. There are 6 _____ in Roger's family, including Roger.

_____ many pancakes will _____ person get?

4. Ino brings _____ to the ballpark. Hot dogs _____

$2.00 each. How _____ hot dogs _____ he _____?

5. It is 42 miles _____ Otterville to Whistlepig. If Jan can travel 7

_____ a day on her skateboard, how many _____ will it

_____ her to _____ to Whistlepig from _____?

6. Lana is organizing _____ books. Her _____ has 6

_____. She has 48 _____. _____ many

books can she put on each shelf?

Division Pick-the-Question

For each word problem beginning sentence, choose the end question that would fit best to make a division problem.

1. Jada has 63 animal erasers.

  a. How many erasers should she put in each box?

  b. How many erasers does she have all together?

  c. How many more erasers does she have than Sara?

  d. How many rabbit erasers does she have?

2. Carly bakes cookies for her dad's birthday.

  a. How many cookies are left?

  b. How many cookies does she bake all together?

  c. How many cookies go on each tray?

  d. How many more cookies does John have?

3. Pooja collects aluminum cans for her recycling project.

  a. How many more cans does Raju collect?

  b. How many cans fit in each bag?

  c. How many cans does she have all together?

  d. How long does it take to collect the cans?

4. Keith watches Robot Revenge cartoons every afternoon.

  a. How many minutes does he watch all together?

  b. How much more television does Teresa watch?

  c. What time is the show over?

  d. How many minutes long is each cartoon?

5. Gala brings $8.00 to the school supply sale.

  a. How many folders can she buy?

  b. How much more money does Stephanie have?

  c. How much does she have left?

  d. How much does she spend all together?

Name: _____

Understanding "Each" Problems

Most word problems that use the word *each* call for multiplication or division. Read the problems below and circle the word *each*. Write "M" if the problem calls for multiplication or "D" if it calls for division. Then solve the problems.

_____ **1.** Betsy buys 8 boxes of cookies. There are 12 cookies in each box. How many cookies does she buy in all?

_____ **2.** The students at Cherry Hill Elementary School sit in rows for the assembly. There are 6 rows of students and 18 students in each row. How many students are at the assembly?

_____ **3.** Pia's dad bakes cupcakes for her birthday. He bakes 3 trays of cupcakes. There are 9 cupcakes on each tray. How many cupcakes does Pia's dad bake?

_____ **4.** Ulla shares her 15 granola bars with two of her friends. How many granola bars does each kid get, including Ulla?

_____ **5.** John buys 4 baseballs. Each baseball costs $12.50. How much does John spend all together?

_____ **6.** Lily has 48 jelly beans and puts them in piles. Each pile contains 6 jelly beans. How many piles can she make?

Teaching Struggling Readers to Tackle Math Word Problems © 2012 by Audrey Trapolsi, Scholastic Teaching Resources

STRATEGY LESSON

Reading and Understanding Fraction Problems

TEACHER TALK

Tell students: *Mathematicians, today we're going to look at word problems that use fractions. What do you already know about fraction problems? What kinds of situations do we find in fraction problems? What usually happens in these stories?* Possible answers include:

- ◆ Sharing
- ◆ Food that is cut equally, like pizza
- ◆ Groups of things
- ◆ Dividing or splitting things up

READ AND DISCUSS

Distribute copies of Understanding Fraction Problems (page 26) to students. If possible, display a copy on the overhead or interactive whiteboard.

Ask students: *What do you notice about word problems that use fractions?* Students may notice that sometimes the fractions are in number form (such as $\frac{2}{5}$) and sometimes they are in word form (such as *half*). Have students circle the fraction in each problem. Invite students to brainstorm a list of fraction words and write them on the whiteboard or on chart paper.

Next, point out to students that all the questions ask "how many?" Ask: *What kind of answer do the questions want—a number or a fraction?* (A number) Explain to students that not all fraction problems want a number for an answer. Sometimes the question asks for a fraction. Instead of asking for "how many," a question might ask "what fraction?"

Reinforce these concepts by having students continue their guided practice. Photocopy the following reproducibles for students and have them work on the pages over the next few days. Be sure to discuss their answers, reinforcing fraction vocabulary and concepts.

- ◆ Fraction Answer or Number Answer? (page 27)
- ◆ Fraction Picture/Problem Matching (page 28)

Understanding Fraction Problems

In each word problem, circle the fraction. (It might be in number form or in word form.) Then solve the problems.

1. There are 24 students in Mr. Ryan's class. If ¼ of them are boys, how many students are boys?

2. Jenna had 18 chocolate drops in a bag. She ate one-third of them. How many chocolate drops did she eat?

3. Half of Ms. Bryde's class has a goldfish for a pet. Eleven students have a goldfish. How many students are in Ms. Bryde's class?

4. Micah had 20 hockey cards. He gave $^2/_5$ of them to Brian. How many hockey cards did he give to Brian?

Teaching Struggling Readers to Tackle Math Word Problems © 2012 by Audrey Trapolsi, Scholastic Teaching Resources

Name: _____

Fraction Answer or Number Answer?

Write "F" next to the word problems that will have a fraction for an answer. Write "N" to the word problems that will have a whole number for an answer. Solve.

_____ **1.** Gemma has 24 cupcakes for the class party. Half of the cupcakes are chocolate. Half of the remaining cupcakes are vanilla, and $\frac{1}{3}$ of the remaining cupcakes are strawberry shortcake. The rest of the cupcakes are chocolate chip. How many cupcakes are chocolate chip?

_____ **2.** Terrence played a 9-inning game of baseball. Six of the innings were scoreless innings. What fraction of the game was scoreless?

_____ **3.** The Pizza Party Deluxe Pie is half pepperoni, and ¼ mushrooms. The rest of the pizza is plain cheese. What fraction of the pizza is plain cheese?

_____ **4.** Henry had one hour to play outside. He played tag for 30 minutes, rode his bike for 20 minutes, and spent the rest of his time on the swings. What fraction of his hour outside was spent on the swings?

_____ **5.** There are 30 students in Mr. Greene's class. Fifteen students play the violin. Five students play the flute and 7 play the piano. How many students do not play the violin, flute, or piano?

_____ **6.** There are 100 cars in the parking lot. One-quarter of them are blue. One-fifth of the cars are green. Two-fifths of the cars are black. The rest of the cars are red. How many cars are red?

Fraction Picture/Problem Matching

Match each word problem with the fraction diagram that goes with the problem. Write the correct letter in the blank before the problem. Solve.

_____ **1.** Byron shared his sandwich equally with Uri. What fraction of his sandwich did Byron eat?

_____ **2.** Kira and seven of her friends are playing softball. Half of the girls are wearing baseball caps. How many girls are wearing baseball caps?

_____ **3.** Janelle shared her cookie equally with Jenny and Jared. What fraction of her cookie did Janelle eat?

_____ **4.** Eduard goes to the library every day after school but not on the weekend. What fraction of the week does he go to the library?

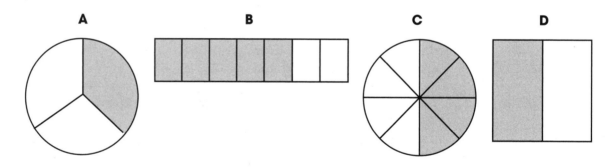

A   B   C   D

Now you shade in the fraction diagram below based on this word problem:

5. David has 6 bottles of juice. He drinks one bottle on Monday and one bottle on Tuesday. What fraction of his juice bottles has David drunk?

STRATEGY LESSON

Reading and Understanding Two-Step Problems

TEACHER TALK

Tell students that in previous lessons, the math problems you've read mostly required just one kind of operation—addition, subtraction, multiplication, or division. But some problems ask us to do two different kinds of operations to find the answer.

READ AND DISCUSS

Distribute copies of Understanding Two-Step Problems reproducible (page 30) to students. If possible, display a copy on the overhead or interactive whiteboard.

Tell students: *Here are five word problems. Three of them are two-step problems.* Read the problems aloud. Ask: *In which problems would we have to do two operations before we get the right answer?* (Questions 1, 3, and 4 are two-step problems.) *Tell me what you notice about how these problems are written. What do these stories have in common?*

Explain to students that these word problems are a little more complicated than single-step problems. They contain more information. Reread the questions in the problems (or ask a volunteer to read them). Say: *I'm noticing that the questions sound a lot like the word-problem questions we have read before in other problems. Who can find a math clue word?* (Let students identify the math clue words they notice, such as *more* or *give*.) Explain that those clue words in the questions can help us figure out the second step in our problem solving, so now we need to figure out what the first step would be. We can do this by looking carefully again at the first part of each problem.

Reread the question from the first word problem. Say: *I notice that this question is talking about "how many more." What kind of math operation does that make you think about?* (Subtraction) *The problem probably needs subtraction. But what am I going to subtract? Let's reread the rest of the problem and figure it out.* Ask students to reread the rest of the problem silently. Then continue: *I see that Bryanna is packing books in boxes. We know that she has packed 8 boxes and that there are 10 books are in each box. The word* each *tells us to multiply. Which numbers do we multiply?* (8 and 10) *So after we multiply, we'll need to subtract the books already packed, 80, from the total she needs to pack, 200. Work together with your neighbor to do that math and then show me when you have an answer.* Invite students to share their answers to make sure most are on track. Then challenge them to solve the other problems.

Have students continue their guided practice. Photocopy the following reproducibles for students and have them work on the pages over the next few days. Be sure to discuss their answers, reinforcing concepts they've already learned.

- ◆ Operation Identification (page 31)
- ◆ Two-Step Problem Fill-In (page 32)

Understanding Two-Step Problems

In which of these problems are there two steps before you find an answer? How do you know? Circle the two-step problems. Underneath each problem, explain how you know it's a two-step problem. Then solve the problems.

1. Bryanna needs to pack 200 books into boxes. So far, she has packed 8 boxes of books. There are 10 books in each box. How many more books does she need to pack?

2. Randall is racing in the Multiple Challenge Race on Saturday. He has to run for 100 yards, hop for 25 yards, ride his bike for 2,000 yards, and swim for 250 yards. How long is the entire race?

3. Jamil has 400 Soccer Star cards. He gives 100 of them to his best friend, George. He shares the rest equally with his brother. How many does Jamil give to his brother?

4. On Wednesday, Thursday, and Friday, Etta made a total of $27 as a dog walker. She made $12 on Wednesday. On Thursday, she made $8. How much did she make on Friday?

5. Jeffrey can do 254 jumps on his pogo stick without stopping. Harry can do 291 jumps on his pogo stick without stopping. Wesley can do 312 jumps without stopping. How many more jumps can Wesley do than Jeffrey?

Operation Identification

Under each problem, circle the letter next to the two operations you need to use to get to the answer. When you are done, compare your answers with your neighbor's and work together to solve all the problems.

1. At the school supply sale, Amos bought an eraser for 75 cents and a special pencil for $1.50. He gave the cashier a $5 bill. How much change did he get back?

    a. Addition and multiplication

    b. Addition and subtraction

    c. Multiplication and subtraction

    d. Division and addition

2. Jenny is also shopping at the school supply sale. She buys four folders for 50 cents each and a jumbo eraser for $1. How much does she spend in all?

    a. Multiplication and addition

    b. Addition and subtraction

    c. Subtraction and multiplication

    d. Addition and division

3. Petra needs 20 yards of fabric for her art project. She buys 4 yards of red fabric and 7 yards of blue fabric. How much more fabric does she need?

    a. Addition and subtraction

    b. Multiplication and addition

    c. Multiplication and subtraction

    d. Addition and division

4. Kendall mowed 4 lawns for $6 each. Kyla earned $20 walking dogs. How much more money did Kendall earn?

    a. Addition and subtraction

    b. Multiplication and addition

    c. Division and subtraction

    d. Multiplication and subtraction

Two-Step Problem Fill-in

Use the word bank to fill in each blank with the correct word or number. Then solve the problems.

WORD BANK

1. Kelly needs 28 juice _____ for her class party. She _____

has _____ apple juice boxes and 8 _____ juice boxes.

How many _____ juice boxes _____ she _____?

> more
> need
> does
> grape
> already
> boxes
> 4

2. Preston has 18 _____ for his bike helmet. He gives 3 to his

_____ and then _____ 7 _____ with his allowance.

How _____ decals does he have _____?

> decals
> more
> brother
> buys
> many
> now

3. Diego _____ $35.00 to buy a new video game. He earns $18

_____ leaves for his neighbors. He spends _____ on

the new Wild Animals _____. How _____ more

does he need to _____ the video game?

> magazine
> much
> buy
> raking
> needs
> $6

4. Gianna _____ 32 cat _____ and 19 dog stickers.

_____ sister Ella has _____ stickers. _____

many more stickers does Ella _____?

> stickers
> How
> have
> 95
> Her
> has

5. Josef's cat weighs twice as _____ as Kevin's cat.

_____ cat weighs 9 _____. How much

_____ the two cats _____ all _____?

> weigh
> pounds
> Kevin's
> much
> do
> together

STRATEGY LESSON

Word Problems With Word Answers

TEACHER TALK

Tell students: *Mathematicians, most of the math problems that we have read and talked about so far have a number for an answer. Today we are going to look at math problems that have word answers.* Ask: *Why would a math problem have a word for an answer? What kinds of words would you expect to find in an answer? What kinds of problems use words for an answer?* Possible answers include:

- ◆ Yes or no problems
- ◆ Problems where the answer is someone's name
- ◆ Problems where you have to choose between things

READ AND DISCUSS

Distribute copies of Understanding Word-Answer Problems (page 34) to students. If possible, display a copy on the overhead or interactive whiteboard.

Focus students' attention on the questions contained in these problems. Ask: *What do you notice about the questions in these word problems?* (The questions don't ask "how many" or "how much" or anything that requires a number answer.) Look at the first question together with the class. Ask: *What kind of answer does the question require?* (Yes or no) Explain to students that they still need to perform math in order to answer the question, but the question itself doesn't ask for the number answer. Go over the rest of the problems with the class, asking volunteers to give the word answer to each problem.

Photocopy the Think About the Answer! reproducible (page 35) and distribute to students. Be sure to discuss their answers, reinforcing concepts they've already learned.

Understanding Word-Answer Problems

Each of these problems requires a word answer instead of numbers. Write the word answer each question is asking for. Solve the problems.

1. Eileen wants to buy 4 chocolate chip cookies for 75 cents each. She has $3.00. Does Eileen have enough money to buy the cookies?

2. Owen, Petra, and Lorenzo run in a race. Petra beat Lorenzo but not Owen. Who won the race?

3. Donal has more stuffed animals than George but fewer than Cinda. Who has the fewest stuffed animals?

4. The watermelon-flavored taffy is 50 cents per piece. The lime-flavored taffy is $3.96 for a box of 12 pieces. Which taffy is the better deal?

Teaching Struggling Readers to Tackle Math Word Problems © 2012 by Audrey Trapolsi, Scholastic Teaching Resources

Think About the Answer!

Read each word problem question. What do you predict about the answer?
Circle the best description of the answer.

1. How many fruit snacks does each student get?

    a. The answer will be a number.

    b. The answer will be yes or no.

    c. The answer will be someone's name.

    d. The answer will be an amount of money.

2. Does Caitlin have enough money to buy the magazine?

    a. The answer will be a number.

    b. The answer will be yes or no.

    c. The answer will be someone's name.

    d. The answer will be an amount of money.

3. How much does each sandwich cost?

    a. The answer will be a number.

    b. The answer will be yes or no.

    c. The answer will be someone's name.

    d. The answer will be an amount of money.

4. Who won the race?

    a. The answer will be a number.

    b. The answer will be yes or no.

    c. The answer will be someone's name.

    d. The answer will be an amount of money.

5. How many dogs does Patrick walk on Saturday?

    a. The answer will be a number.

    b. The answer will be yes or no.

    c. The answer will be someone's name.

    d. The answer will be an amount of money.

6. Does Hector have enough cupcakes for the whole class?

    a. The answer will be a number.

    b. The answer will be yes or no.

    c. The answer will be someone's name.

    d. The answer will be an amount of money.

Extended-Response Problem Reading

TEACHER TALK

Tell students: *By now, you have a basic understanding of what key words and phrases to look for in word problems. This should help you tackle regular math word problems. However, most standardized math tests include extended-response problems.* Explain that the most important part of attacking these problems is to recognize that they contain more than one question. Many proficient math students lose critical points on these test items because they answer one part of the problem completely and correctly, but then do not complete the remaining parts of the question. Students need to remember that these problems have multiple parts and to identify what those parts are.

READ AND DISCUSS

Distribute copies of Amy, the Eraser Ace (page 37) to students. If possible, display a copy on the overhead or interactive whiteboard.

Invite a student volunteer to read aloud the problem on the page. Then ask students: *What do you notice about this problem?* (The problem requires more than one answer.) Tell students that when they come across this type of problem, they should keep in mind these key ideas:

1. The first bullet point or question item is usually the easiest. It is typically a fairly straightforward problem-solving question. Ask students: *What type of answer is this first question looking for?* (A yes or no answer) Point out the second part of the question, which asks students to explain their answer or show their work. Explain that a simple "yes" or "no" is not sufficient. They have to show how they figured out their answer.

2. Subsequent bullet points require more complex responses that require students to show higher-level thinking, such as comparing, identifying a pattern, constructing (a graph, pattern, or other math object), and generalizing. For this problem, students need to show two ways Amy could give Eric the correct change. Invite students to share their ideas.

Finally, tell students that even if their answers to all parts are not completely correct, they can often earn valuable partial credit on these problems if they demonstrate some understanding, by explaining with the use of words, pictures, or numbers. Students usually have a significant amount of time to tackle these problems and many finish early. That extra time can help boost scores if students learn another way to prove their answer is correct, or support their answer with drawings and explanations.

Give students more practice with these types of problems by photocopying and distributing the following reproducibles. Tell students that, like actual test items, these practice problems feature more than one bulleted task. By reading all tasks carefully and identifying the math they need to do, students can make the most of their allotted time.

- Yolanda's Garden Area (page 38)
- Spinning Sarah (page 39)

Name: _____

Amy, the Eraser Ace

Amy is selling some of her erasers to her friends.
Each eraser costs 40 cents. Eric buys two erasers
and gives Amy a one-dollar bill. Amy gives Eric 10
cents in change.

• Did Amy give Eric the correct change? Explain
  your answer or show your work.

• Show two ways that Amy could give Eric the
  correct change.

Yolanda's Garden Area

Yolanda planted two gardens, A and B, in her backyard.

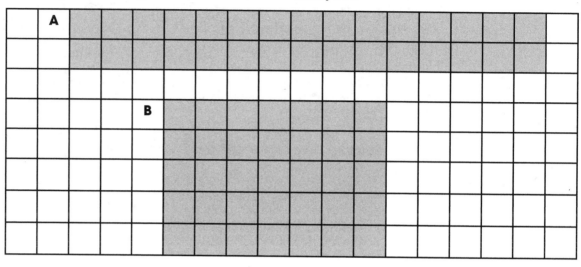

☐ **One square unit**

• Determine the perimeter of each garden.

• Which garden has the greater area? Explain your answer.

Spinning Sarah

- What is the probability of spinning a 2 on spinner A?

- Sarah wins if she spins an even number. Which spinner should she spin to have the best chance of winning? Explain your answer.

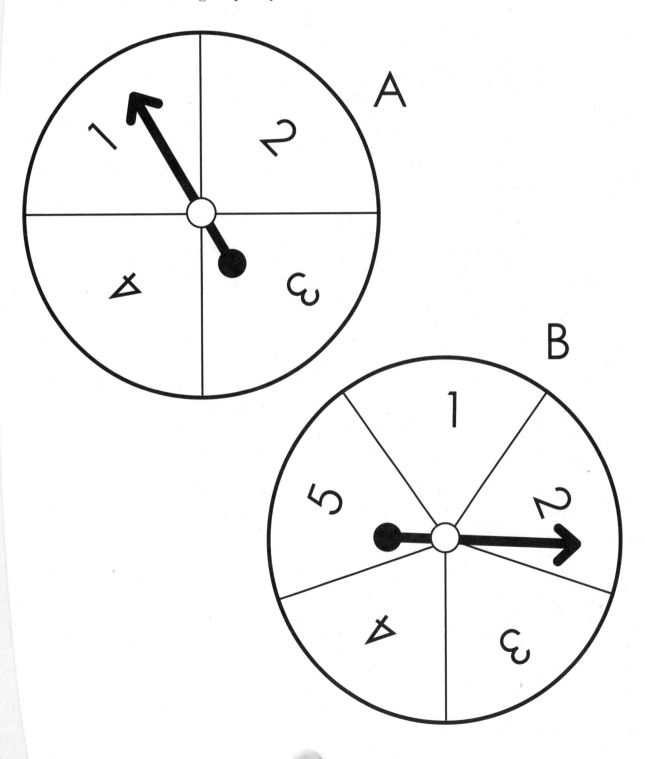

STRATEGY LESSON

Creating Word Problems

TEACHER TALK

Tell students: *So far we've looked at different kinds of word problems and talked about various strategies for reading and solving them. This time, however, you are going to create your own word problems. This will also help you figure out what kinds of information to look for in a problem.*

READ AND DISCUSS

Distribute copies of Word Problem Info Hunt (page 41) to students. If possible, display a copy on the overhead or interactive whiteboard.

Write the following problem on the board for students:

> *Keira went to the store to buy some supplies for an art project. She bought construction paper for $1.00, colored markers for $2.50, and glitter glue for $3.25. How much did she spend in all?*

Give students some time to read over the problem silently. Then divide the class into small groups and ask students to work with their group to fill in the Word Problem Info Hunt. After several minutes, call on volunteers from each group to share their answers with the class. Explain to students that whenever they encounter word problems, they should automatically look for the information listed on the sheet. This will help them solve any problem.

Give students more practice understanding the structure of word problems by photocopying and distributing the following reproducibles. On these worksheets, students will identify key information in word problems, write their own problems, and put sentences and pictures in logical order so the problems make sense. Have them work on the pages over the next few days, and discuss their answers.

- ◆ Highlighter Hunt (page 42)
- ◆ Story Starters (page 43)
- ◆ Picture Problems (page 44)
- ◆ Scrambled Sentences (page 45)
- ◆ Scrambled Pictures (page 46)

Word Problem Info Hunt

Anytime you have to solve a word problem, find the answers to these questions. Knowing this information will help you solve the problem.

1. Who is the problem about?

2. What is he/she doing?

3. What numbers does the problem give us?

4. What units does the problem use?

5. Copy the question from the problem.

6. What do you need to figure out?

7. Your answer will be a (circle one): number, word, name, yes/no

8. What operation will this problem use?

9. How can you prove that your answer is correct?

Highlighter Hunt

You will need four highlighters: pink, yellow, green, and orange.

Read each word problem below and use your highlighters to color important information in the problem:

- Find the question in the problem. Highlight the question in yellow.
- Find who the problem is about. Highlight this in green.
- Find what the person is doing in the problem. Highlight the activity in pink.
- Find the numbers in the problem that you will need to solve the problem. Highlight the numbers in orange.
- Use your pencil to draw a circle around the math clue words that tell you what operation you will need to use to solve the problem.
- Find the one multiplication problem on the page and solve it.

1. Petra collects stickers. She gets 225 stickers from her parents for her birthday. She gets 175 stickers from her sister Sami. How many stickers does she have in all?

2. It is Field Day at Town Center Elementary School. Darien jumps 4 feet, 4 inches in the long-jump contest. Josephine jumps 50 inches. Who jumped farther?

3. The students in Ms. Birrer's class sit in rows. Each row has 5 student desks. There are 5 rows. How many students are in Ms. Birrer's class?

Teaching Struggling Readers to Tackle Math Word Problems © 2012 by Audrey Trapolsi, Scholastic Teaching Resources

Story Starters

For each of the beginning sentences below, write a word problem. Write a number sentence that goes with your word problem. Give your problem to a partner to solve.

1. James keeps his baseball cards in boxes of 100.

2. Destinee earns $4.00 to walk the dog.

3. Lin bought three books at the book fair.

4. Latika needs $150 to buy an UltraGame video game system.

5. It is 237 miles from Bubbletown to Zippyville.

Picture Problems

Cut out pictures from magazines, catalogs, or newspapers and glue them below to make a story problem. Make sure you include a picture for every step of your problem. On the back of this page, write an equation and a word problem that goes with your picture problem. Solve.

Teaching Struggling Readers to Tackle Math Word Problems © 2012 by Audrey Trapolsi, Scholastic Teaching Resources

Scrambled Sentences

Make a word problem by putting the sentences in order. Write the order number in front of each sentence. On a separate sheet of paper, draw a picture to illustrate one of the word problems. Write an equation to match the word problem. Solve.

1. _____ How many weeks will it take until Sophie can buy the softball glove?
_____ Sophie walks the dogs 5 days a week.
_____ The softball glove that Sophie wants costs $40.
_____ Sophie makes $3 a day walking dogs.

2. _____ For dessert, he bought a lollipop shaped like a baseball for $1.25.
_____ Next, he bought orange juice for 75 cents.
_____ First, he bought a hamburger for $1.50.
_____ How much change did Jimmy give his mom?
_____ Jimmy's mom gave him $5.00 to buy lunch.

3. _____ How many gummi worms does Jin have?
_____ Jin puts 10 gummi worms in each bag.
_____ She has 3 bags of gummi worms.

4. _____ She gives 14 to her best friend.
_____ Amy has 50 Sparkle Ghost game cards.
_____ How many cards does she have left?
_____ Then, she gives 8 to her sister.

5. _____ How many boxes will Pranathi need?
_____ Pranathi has 40 cupcakes she needs to take to school.
_____ She can fit 6 cupcakes in each box.

6. _____ Boxes of 5 candy bars are $3.00.
_____ Which is the better deal?
_____ Candy bars are 75 cents each.
_____ Akhil wants to buy 10 candy bars.

These sentences form two word problems. Cut out the sentence strips. Sort the sentences and put them in order. Then, on the back of this page, illustrate them, write matching equations, and solve.

| It is now four o'clock in the afternoon. |
| Petra puts 3 gumballs in each goodie bag for her party. |
| How long has she been at the library? |
| Jennifer got to the library at 2:30 p.m. |
| How many gumballs will she need? |
| There are 8 children coming to her party. |

Name: _____

Scrambled Pictures

Cut out each set of pictures and put them in order to make a math story. On a separate sheet of paper, write a word problem that would go with this story. Also write an equation that would go with your word problem.

Mastery Activities

Once students are comfortable with word problems using the four different operations, use these reproducibles and activities to provide them with advanced practice and opportunities for higher-level logic and thinking.

In the first three reproducibles—Equation Matching (page 48), Matching the Equation to the Situation (page 49), and What's the Equation? (page 50)—students match a word problem with an equation. These will help you assess how well they truly understand what a word problem is asking for. Beginning to End (page 51) gives students the first sentence of a word problem and asks them to predict what an appropriate question might follow. In What's Missing? (page 52), students figure out what vital piece of information they need in order to solve the word problem.

The rest of this section offers activities that students can do either in pairs or in small groups. The activities include a word problem scavenger hunt (page 53), a create-your-own-story-problem activity (page 57), and several whole-class and small-group games.

Enjoy!

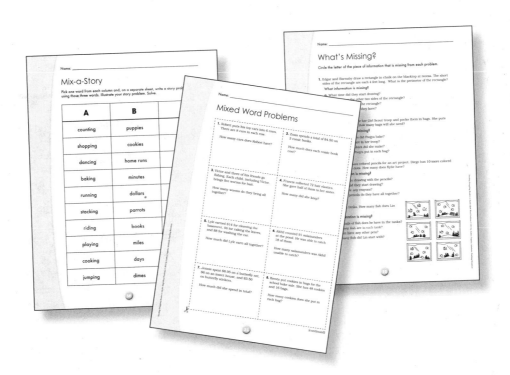

Equation Matching

Match each word problem with the correct equation. Solve

1. There were 28 tables at the book fair. The tables were arranged in rows of 4. How many tables were in each row?

    a. 28 x 4 = ?

    b. 4 + ? = 28

    c. 28 ÷ 4 = ?

    d. 8 – 4 = ?

2. George wants to make vases of flowers for the Mother's Day sale. He wants to put 12 flowers in every vase. He has 96 flowers. How many vases can he make?

    a. 96 ÷ 12 = ?

    b. 12 x 96 = ?

    c. 96 – 12 = ?

    d. 12 + ? = 96

3. Kirsten is making bags of cookies for the school bake sale. She has 45 cookies. She needs 15 bags of cookies. How many cookies can she put in each bag?

    a. 45 – 15 = ?

    b. 15 + ? = 45

    c. 15 ÷ 45 = ?

    d. 45 ÷ 15 = ?

4. Ty can put 8 baseball cards in each page of his baseball card album. He has 67 baseball cards. How many pages will he need for his collection?

    a. 67 ÷ 8 = ?

    b. 8 + 67 = ?

    c. 67 x 8 = ?

    d. 67 – 8 = ?

Teaching Struggling Readers to Tackle Math Word Problems © 2012 by Audrey Trapolsi, Scholastic Teaching Resources

Matching the Equation to the Situation

Circle the letter of the math situation that could match each number sentence. Solve.

1. 235 + 897 =

    a. Natalie wants to find out how many stickers she has all together.

    b. Natalie wants to know if she has more stickers than Jume.

    c. Natalie wants to put her stickers in equal groups.

    d. Natalie wants to sell her stickers.

2. 12 x 3 =

    a. Owen gives some of his baseball cards to Carlos and wants to know how many he has left.

    b. Owen puts his baseball cards in groups and wants to know how many he has all together.

    c. Owen lost some of his baseball cards and wants to count how many he has now.

    d. Owen needs to share his baseball cards evenly with his brother.

3. 24 ÷ 4 =

    a. Hala gives some of her pencils to Sarah and wants to know how many she has left.

    b. Hala wants to see how many pencils she has in all.

    c. Hala wants to share her pencils with her friends.

    d. Hala wants to give half her pencils to her teacher.

4. 83 – 25 =

    a. Logan puts some jelly beans in even piles and wants to know how many are in each pile.

    b. Logan wants to share his jelly beans evenly with some of his friends.

    c. Logan gives some of his jelly beans to his brother and wants to know how many he has left.

    d. Logan wants to know how many jelly beans he has all together.

What's the Equation?

Circle the letter of the number sentence that goes with each word problem. Solve.

1. Hector wants to buy a new bicycle helmet that costs $80. He has saved $20.
How much more money does he need to buy the helmet?

    a. $80 − $20 = ?

    b. $80 + $20 = ?

    c. $100 − $20 = ?

    d. $80 ÷ $20 = ?

2. Lianna shares a box of popsicles with three of her friends. There are 12 popsicles in
the box and 4 girls (including Lianna). How many popsicles does each girl get?

    a. 12 − 4 = ?

    b. 12 ÷ 4 = ?

    c. 4 + 4 = ?

    d. ¼ x 4 = ?

3. There are 6 cards in every pack of Extreme Shark Team collector cards.
Tim buys 7 packs of cards. How many cards does he have?

    a. 7 − 6 = ?

    b. $^6/_7 + {}^7/_6$ = ?

    c. 7 x 6 = ?

    d. 7 ÷ 6 = ?

4. Janella plants 10 sunflowers
in every row in her garden.
There are 6 rows.
How many sunflowers does
she plant all together?

    a. 6 x 10 = ?

    b. 60 − 10 = ?

    c. 10 + 6 = ?

    d. 10 ÷ 6 = ?

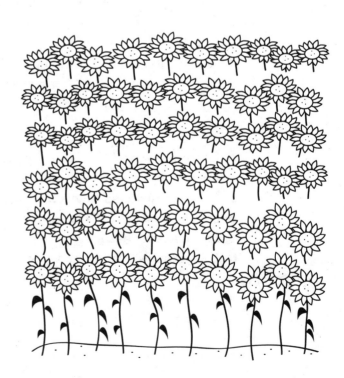

Beginning to End

Match the first sentence in each word problem with the question that could go with it. Write the letter of the question in the blank next to the correct sentence.

_____ **1.** Paul brings cookies to school for his class party.

_____ **2.** Scott is baking trays of cookies.

_____ **3.** Ira buys cookies for a party at school.

_____ **4.** Akhil is sharing cookies with three of his friends.

_____ **5.** Roberto has 18 cookies.

A. How many cookies does he have left?

B. How many cookies does each child get?

C. Does he have enough money?

D. How many cookies does he have in all?

E. How many cookies are on each tray?

Name: _____

What's Missing?

Circle the letter of the piece of information that is missing from each problem.

1. Edgar and Barnaby draw a rectangle in chalk on the blacktop at recess. The short sides of the rectangle are each 4 feet long. What is the perimeter of the rectangle?

What information is missing?

   a. What time did they start drawing?

   b. How long are the other two sides of the rectangle?

   c. Where do they draw the rectangle?

   d. How much chalk do they have?

2. Poojya bakes cookies for her Girl Scout troop and packs them in bags. She puts 4 cookies in each bag. How many bags will she need?

What information is missing?

   a. How many cookies did Poojya bake?

   b. How many girls are in her troop?

   c. What kind of cookies did she make?

   d. How many did Poojya put in each bag?

3. Kylie and Diego share colored pencils for an art project. Diego has 10 more colored pencils than Kylie does. How many does Kylie have?

What information is missing?

   a. What are they drawing with the pencils?

   b. What time did they start drawing?

   c. Do they have any crayons?

   d. How many pencils do they have all together?

4. Lin has 6 fish tanks. How many fish does Lin have in all?

What information is missing?

   a. What kinds of fish does he have in the tanks?

   b. How many fish are in each tank?

   c. Does Lin have any other pets?

   d. How many fish did Lin start with?

Mixed Word Problems

Two separate activities can be based on the Mixed Word Problems reproducibles that follow (pages 55–56). They are both great review activities after you've covered the four main mathematical operations.

1. OPERATIONS ORGANIZER

Photocopy and distribute Operations Organizer (page 54) to each pair of students. If possible, display a copy on the overhead or interactive whiteboard. Also make copies of Mixed Word Problems for each pair. Have students cut out the individual word-problem cards and display them in front of them.

Tell students: *Now that we've learned how to read word problems with four different kinds of operations, let's see how much we remember. You have 16 word-problem cards in front of you, and four columns on your organizer sheet, labeled* Addition, Subtraction, Multiplication, *and* Division. *Read through the problems and sort the cards according to the operation. What are you going to look for to find your addition problems? What about multiplication problems?*

2. WORD PROBLEM SCAVENGER HUNT

Divide the class into small groups so that students can support one another's reading. Give each group a copy of the Scavenger Hunt Directions (below) and the Mixed Word Problems. You can also use word problems from other sources, such as this book, old corrected homework papers, and students' textbook (have students copy the word problems they find instead of cutting them out).

Stop students after about 20 minutes or when you observe that they have either found most of their items or are having some difficulty. Ask students to share where they found their word problems and, most importantly, how they could tell that a problem fit the description on their scavenger hunt list. For example: *How did you know you had found a two-step problem? How did you know that a problem uses multiplication?*

Scavenger Hunt Directions

Read the clues below. Look for a word problem that matches each description. Then label the problem with the letter it matches.

a. A problem about money

b. A problem that uses the words *How many*

c. A problem about time

d. A problem that uses multiplication

e. A problem that uses subtraction

f. A two-step problem

g. A problem has a word answer

Name: _____

Operations Organizer

ADDITION	SUBTRACTION	MULTIPLICATION	DIVISION

Mixed Word Problems

1. Robert puts his toy cars into 6 rows. There are 8 cars in each row.

How many cars does Robert have?

2. Zosia spends a total of $4.50 on 3 comic books.

How much does each comic book cost?

3. Victor and three of his friends go fishing. Each child, including Victor, brings five worms for bait.

How many worms do they bring all together?

4. Francie collected 72 hair elastics. She gave $1/6$ of them to her sister.

How many did she keep?

5. Lyle earned $14 for cleaning the basement, $6 for raking the leaves, and $8 for washing the car.

How much did Lyle earn all together?

6. Akhil counted 91 salamanders at the pond. He was able to catch 18 of them.

How many salamanders was Akhil unable to catch?

7. Jennie spent $8.95 on a butterfly net, $6 on an insect house, and $3.50 on butterfly stickers.

How much did she spend in total?

8. Kersta put cookies in bags for the school bake sale. She has 48 cookies and 16 bags.

How many cookies does she put in each bag?

(continued)

Mixed Word Problems (continued)

9. Yuri puts 20 books on each shelf. There are 6 shelves in the bookcase.

How many books can Yuri fit in the bookcase?

10. Calla brings juice boxes to the party. There are 3 juice boxes in each pack. She brings 9 packs.

How many juice boxes does she bring in all?

11. Kevin can fit 6 lunch bags into every backpack.

If there are 40 lunch bags, how many backpacks will he need to carry them all?

12. Addison bought a pack of sunflower seeds for $1.60. There are 10 seeds in the pack.

How much does each seed cost?

13. James is allowed to watch 90 minutes of television each week. Tonight he watched 35 minutes of television.

How many more minutes of television can he watch for the rest of the week?

14. Eva earned 12,500 points in level one of her Galaxy Penguin game. She earned 8,750 points in level two and 5,600 points in level three.

What was her final score?

15. Mei needs to score 26,500 points in her Kitten Veterinarian game to get the high score. She scored 17,900 in level one.

How much does she need to score in level two?

16. Cedric sells all 7 of his Frog Agent action figures for $3.50 each.

How much money does he make?

Mix-a-Story

Creating their own word problems will help students solidify their understanding of math reading concepts. List the following words on the board:

Stacking
Riding
Playing
Cooking
Jumping

To begin the whole-class discussion, pick one word from the list and ask students: *How could we use this word in a word problem? What kinds of math would that problem involve?* Record students' suggestions on the board. Pair up students, then ask each pair to pick a word from the list. Have students discuss with their partner how their word could be included in a word problem.

Photocopy the Mix-a-Story reproducible (page 58) and cut apart the words. Divide the class into small groups and give each group a word from each column (each group should get three words). Have each group brainstorm a word problem using their three words. Encourage students to illustrate their group's word problem and include a number sentence to accompany the written problem.

For homework or independent practice, distribute copies of the Write Your Own! reproducible (page 59). Invite students to share the problems they wrote with the class and challenge them to solve the problems.

Mix-a-Story

Pick one word from each column and, on a separate sheet, write a story problem using those three words. Illustrate your story problem. Solve.

A	B	C
counting	puppies	each
shopping	cookies	every
dancing	home runs	long
baking	minutes	many
running	dollars	does
stacking	parrots	all
riding	books	far
playing	miles	tall
cooking	days	much
jumping	dimes	how

Teaching Struggling Readers to Tackle Math Word Problems © 2012 by Audrey Traposit, Scholastic Teaching Resources

Write Your Own!

1. Write a word problem that will have "yes" as an answer.

2. Write a word problem that will have "no" as an answer.

3. Write a word problem that will have "Kristen" as an answer.

4. Write a word problem that will have "The Eagles" as an answer.

5. Write a word problem that will have "4th grade boys" as an answer.

Whole-Class and Small-Group Games and Activities

MATH CHARADES

This super-fun game can be played as a whole class or in small groups. Play this game to review or reinforce students' understanding of math operation "situations," specifically when to use addition, subtraction, multiplication, and/or division.

Before the game, write the four math operations on separate index cards: "Addition," "Subtraction," "Multiplication," and "Division." If you have divided the class into groups, make a set of operation cards for each group.

To play, have each student choose an operation card. Tell the student not to show the card to the class. On a separate index card, have the student write a word problem that uses the operation. Then, in front of the class or group, have the student silently act out his or her math problem. If another student guesses what is going on in the math story—for example, shopping for groceries—and correctly identifies which operation is being used in the first student's word problem, he or she goes next. When a student identifies the charade activity, make sure he or she explains *why* he or she thinks the problem is an addition problem, for example.

Record the depicted activities and the associated operations in a table on chart paper or your whiteboard. For example:

ACTIVITY	MATH	OPERATION
cooking	putting cookies in groups	multiplication
baseball	scoring runs	addition
playing video games	comparing scores	subtraction

After you have played several rounds, discuss with students what they notice about the activities on the chart and what kind of math they used.

MATH STORY CHAIN

This activity works best with a group of six to eight students. Alternatively, you can put the whole class in groups that work together. Have one student write the first sentence of a math problem on the board. Select a different student to write the next sentence. Students continue to write the word problem, one sentence at a time. When they think they can solve the problem, students indicate by showing a special signal, such as two fingers in the air. Invite a student volunteer to write his or her solution on the board. Discuss with the group whether they agree with this solution and whether there are other possible answers.

TEAM WORD PROBLEM UNSCRAMBLE

Make two copies of a word problem on sentence strips—one sentence on each strip. To make the game even more challenging, add one or two sentences from another word problem that don't belong. Divide the class into two teams. Challenge the two teams to unscramble the word problem and arrange their sentence strips on the board or table. When students think they are finished, have them read the unscrambled problem. Discuss: *How did you put the sentences in order? How would you solve it?*

OPERATION IDENTIFICATION

Have each student make four cards, one for each operational symbol (÷, ×, +, −). Read aloud word problems from the Mixed Word Problems reproducible pages (pages 55–56) or any other source, or have students share problems they have written. As soon as students can identify the operation used in the problem, they should hold up the correct card. Discuss: *How did you know what operation you'd use?* If there is disagreement, discuss all student suggestions.

TEAM WORD PROBLEM RELAY

Use the Mix-a-Story cards from column C (page 58) for this activity. Divide the class into three or four teams. Each team gets a small whiteboard or space on an easel or writing surface that the class can see. Pick one card at random and show all teams. The first person on each team writes a word problem on his/her whiteboard that uses that math vocabulary word. The next player on each team solves the problem and sits down when finished. Review each team's word problems before continuing to the next round. Discuss similarities and differences among the teams' different problems. Play continues after review with the second person on each team writing a word problem that uses a second vocabulary word, which is then solved by the third person on the team.

WEEKEND NEWS MATH

Invite students to share what they did the previous weekend. Turn those experiences into word problems—what math could happen at a birthday party? At the mall? At a soccer game?

VIDEO GAME PROBLEMS

For this activity, divide the class into small groups. Within each group have students describe their favorite video games. Pick one game to work with. Ask: *What math happens in the game?* Compare and describe the math that happens in video games, such as adding points, bonuses that multiply scores, and so on. Have students illustrate their video game examples.

MATH MATCH

Students can play this game in pairs or small groups. Cut apart the cards on page 62 and place them facedown. At his or her turn, a player turns over two cards at a time. If the math question on one card fits the answer on the other card, the player keeps both cards. If the cards don't match, the next player gets a turn. The player with the most cards at the end of the game wins.

How many cupcakes will Sabrina need in all?	24 cupcakes	What time will the movie be over?
4:30 p.m.	How far did they travel?	4 miles
How much taller is Mai than Annie?	3 centimeters	Will Brian have enough money to buy the skateboard?
Yes	How much change will Jeremy receive?	$2.50
How much time will you have to ride the roller coaster?	30 minutes	How many boxes will Thomas need?
10 boxes	Did Micah spend more on toy cars or on toy trucks?	Toy cars
How old is Jamie's little sister?	Four years old	How wide is Jan's living room?
20 feet	How many times can Ulla ride the merry-go-round?	Twice

Answers

PAGE 7: Understanding Addition Problems

Problems 1 and 4 use addition. A signal from problem 1 is the phrase *all together*. In problem 4, money amounts are being combined.

Answers:
1. 85 cards
2. 58 jelly beans
3. 5 groups
4. 85 cents

PAGE 8: Addition Draw-It

Students should draw 3 balloons plus 1 balloon, for a total of 4 balloons, and then write it as 3 + 1 = 4.
Students should draw 8 smiley faces plus 7 smiley faces, for a total of 15 smiley faces, and then write it as 8 + 7 = 15.

PAGE 9: Addition Fill-In

The filled-in words and numbers, in the correct order:
1. points, scored, game, many, all [Answer: 380 points]
2. fruit, bought, watermelon, six, How, did, in [12 pieces of fruit]
3. cupcakes, vanilla, 4, bring, together [24 cupcakes]
4. collects, 19, books, comic, does, have [58 comic books]

PAGE 10: Addition Pick-the-Question

1. b [Answer: 27 animals]
2. c [$24]
3. d [6 runs]
4. b [7 hours]
5. a [21,500 points]

PAGE 12: Understanding Multiplication Problems

Problems 3 and 5 use multiplication. Clue words in problem 3 are *each* and *in all*. In problem 5, *each* and *all together* signal multiplication.

Answers:
1. 89 more fifth graders
2. 45 minutes
3. $3.56
4. $3.20
5. 120 ounces
6. Fernando's, by 30 feet

PAGE 13: Visual Organizer: Comparing Addition and Multiplication

Answers will vary. Overlapping words might include *all together, total, more, bigger*.

PAGE 14: Multiplication Fill-In

The filled-in words and numbers, in the correct order:
1. 3, every, class, airplanes, make, all [Answer: 39 airplanes]
2. pet, times, as, 200, have [1,000 goldfish]
3. pounds, costs, much, spend [$27]
4. bags, camping, Each, How, weigh [24 pounds]

PAGE 16: Understanding Subtraction Problems

Problems 2 and 3 use subtractions. Clue words in problem 2 are *gave* and *left*. In problem 3, *farther* signals subtraction.

Answers:
1. $21.50
2. 117 comic books
3. 19 miles farther
4. 4 hours, 15 minutes

PAGE 17: Subtraction Pick-the-Question

1. b [Answer: 24 more girls]
2. a [4 more feet]
3. b [45 more seconds]
4. b [5 more feet]
5. b [6 more ounces]
6. a [1 yard and 1 foot more]

PAGE 18: Subtraction Fill-In

The filled-in words and numbers, in the correct order:
1. clip, long, used, paper, How, more, use [Answer: 59 more paper clips]
2. Hilltown, of, boys, many, players [355 girls]
3. points, advance, level, more, score, she, two [7,500 more points]
4. miles, Leaftown, It, to, farther, than [136 more miles]
5. had, stickers, 14, many, Petra, left [67 stickers]
6. pounds, cat, weighs, 6, more, weigh [1 pound, 10 ounces more]

PAGE 19: Equation Matching

1. b [Answer: $1.25]
2. a [$3.50 more]
3. d [$2.60 more]
4. d [12,500 more points]

PAGE 21: Understanding Division Problems

Problems 1 and 4 use division. A clue word in problem 1 is *each*. In problem 4, *each* and *will get the same number* signal division.

Answers:
1. 5 dogs
2. Yes, exactly enough.
3. 151 more pages
4. 5 cookies

PAGE 22: Division Fill-In

The filled-in words and numbers, in the correct order:
1. cars, each, 56, boxes, all [Answer: 8 boxes]
2. 24, class, students, rows, 4, many, each [6 students]
3. cooks, family, 18, people, How, each [3 pancakes]
4. $14.00, cost, many, can, buy [7 hot dogs]
5. from, miles, days, take, go, Otterville [6 days]
6. her, bookcase, shelves, books, How [8 books]

PAGE 23: Division Pick-the-Question

1. a
2. c
3. b
4. d
5. a

PAGE 24: Understanding "Each" Problems

1. M [96 cookies]
2. M [108 students]
3. M [27 cupcakes]
4. D [5 bars]
5. M [$50]
6. D [8 piles]

PAGE 26: Understanding Fraction Problems

1. 1/4 [Answer: 6 students]
2. One-third [6 chocolate drops]
3. Half [22 students]
4. 2/5 [8 hockey cards]

PAGE 27: Fraction Answer or Number Answer?

1. N [Answer: 4 cupcakes]
2. F [2/3]
3. F [1/4]
4. F [1/6]
5. N [3 students]
6. N [15 cars]

PAGE 28: Fraction Picture/Problem Matching

1. D [1/2]
2. C [4/8]
3. A [1/3]
4. B [5/7]
5. [Show the rectangle with 2 of the 6 sections shaded] [2/6]

PAGE 30: Understanding Two-Step Problems

Problems 1, 3, and 4 are two-step problems.
In problem 1, you'd multiply the number of boxes times the number of books in a box. You'd subtract that product from the total number of books.
In problem 3, you'd subtract the cards given to George from the total. Then you'd divide that difference by 2.
In problem 4, you'd add the Wednesday and Thursday amounts. Then you'd subtract that sum from the total earnings. (You could also subtract Wednesday from the total, then subtract Thursday.)

Answers:
1. 120 more books
2. 2,375 yards
3. 150 cards
4. $7
5. 58 more jumps

PAGE 31: Operation Identification

1. b [Answer: $2.75]
2. a [$3]
3. a [9 more yards]
4. d [$4 more]

PAGE 32: Two-Step Problem Fill-In

1. boxes, already, 4, grape, more, does, need [Answer: 16 more boxes]
2. decals, brother, buys, more, many, now [22 decals]
3. needs, raking, $6, magazine, much, buy [$23 more]
4. has, stickers, Her, 95, How, have [44 more stickers]
5. much, Kevin's, pounds, do, weigh, together [27 pounds]

Answers

PAGE 34: Understanding Word Answer Problems

1. a yes or no response [Answer: Yes, exactly enough]
2. a name (person who won the race) [Owen]
3. a name (person with the fewest stuffed animals) [George]
4. a flavor of taffy (the one that is the better deal) [lime, which is $.33 per piece]

PAGE 35: Think About the Answer!

1. a
2. b
3. d
4. c
5. a
6. b

PAGE 37: Amy, the Eraser Ace

- Amy did not give Eric the correct change. Two erasers would cost 80 cents, so Eric should receive 20 cents change from his $1 bill, not 10 cents.
- Answers will vary. Could be pictures of two dimes, one dime and two nickels, etc. It's correct as long as the coins add up to 20 cents!

PAGE 38: Yolanda's Garden Area

- Garden A has a perimeter of 34 units. Garden B has a perimeter of 24 units.
- Garden B has a greater area. Its area is 35 square units, compared with 30 square units for garden A.

PAGE 39: Spinning Sarah

- The probability of spinning a 2 on spinner A is 1/4.
- She should use spinner A. The probability of spinning an even number is 2/4 or 1/2. On spinner B, the probability would be 2/5. The probability is greater on spinner A: 50% vs. 40%.

PAGE 41: Word Problem Info Hunt

1. Keira
2. buying supplies for an art project
3. $1.00, $2.50, $3.25
4. dollars and cents
5. How much did she spend in all?
6. How much money she spent
7. number
8. addition
9. Answers will vary.

PAGE 42: Highlighter Hunt

1. yellow = How many stickers does she have in all?
   green = Petra
   pink = collects stickers
   orange = 225 and 175
   circle around = in all
   [Answer: 400 stickers]
2. yellow = Who jumped farther?
   green = Darien and Josephine
   pink = long-jump contest
   orange = 4 feet, 4 inches and 50 inches
   circle around = farther
   [Answer: Darien, 2 inches farther]
3. yellow = How many students are in Ms. Birrer's class?
   green = students
   pink = sit in rows
   orange = 5 and 5
   circle around = each, How many
   This is the multiplication problem. [Answer: 25 students]

PAGE 43: Story Starters

Answers will vary.

PAGE 44: Picture Problems

Answers will vary. Verify that word problems match equations, and that solutions are accurate.

PAGE 45: Scrambled Sentences

Equations may vary. Order of sentences may vary slightly. Illustrations will vary a lot!

1. The softball glove that Sophie wants costs $40. Sophie makes $3 a day walking dogs. Sophie walks the dogs 5 days a week. How many weeks will it take until Sophie can buy the softball glove?
   $40 ÷ ($3 x 5) = ?
   In 3 weeks, she'll earn $45.
2. Jimmy's mom gave him $5.00 to buy lunch. First, he bought a hamburger for $1.50. Next, he bought orange juice for 75 cents. For dessert, he bought a lollipop shaped like a baseball for $1.25. How much change did Jimmy give his mom?
   $5 – $1.50 – $.75 – $1.25 = ?
   $1.50
3. Jin puts 10 gummi worms in each bag. She has 3 bags of gummi worms.
   How many gummi worms does Jin have?
   10 x 3 = ?
   30 gummi worms

4. Amy has 50 Sparkle Ghost game cards. She gives 14 to her best friend. Then, she gives 8 to her sister. How many cards does she have left?
   50 – 14 – 8 = ?
   28 game cards
5. Pranathi has 40 cupcakes she needs to take to school. She can fit 6 cupcakes in each box. How many boxes will Pranathi need?
   40 ÷ 6 = ?
   She needs 7 boxes.
6. Akhil wants to buy 10 candy bars. Candy bars are 75 cents each. Boxes of 5 candy bars are $3.00. Which is the better deal?
   10 x .75
   2 x $3
   The boxes are a better deal: $6 for 10 bars vs. $7.50 for 10.

Petra puts 3 gumballs in each goodie bag for her party. There are 8 children coming to her party. How many gumballs will she need?
3 x 8 = ?
24 gumballs

Jennifer got to the library at 2:30 p.m. It is now four o'clock in the afternoon. How long has she been at the library?
4:00 – 2:30 = ?
90 minutes (one and a half hours)

PAGE 46: Scrambled Pictures

Order of pictures, equations, and word problems will vary slightly.

1. $5 – $2 – $.50 – $.75 = $1.75
2. 4 x 4 = 16 mittens
3. 4 + 5 + 6 = 15 flowers

PAGE 48: Equation Matching

1. c [Answer: 7 tables]
2. a [8 vases]
3. d [3 cookies]
4. a [9 pages]

PAGE 49: Matching the Equation to the Situation

1. a [Answer: 1,132 stickers]
2. b [36 baseball cards]
3. c [6 pencils]
4. c [58 jelly beans]

PAGE 50: What's the Equation?

1. a [Answer: $60 more]
2. b [3 popsicles]
3. c [42 cards]
4. a [60 sunflowers]

PAGE 51: Beginning to End

1. D
2. E
3. C
4. B
5. A

PAGE 52: What's Missing?

1. b
2. a
3. d
4. b

PAGE 54: Operations Organizer

Addition: 5, 7, 14
Subtraction: 6, 13, 15
Multiplication: 1, 3, 9, 10, 16
Division: 2, 4, 8, 11, 12

PAGES 55–56: Mixed Word Problems

Answers

1. 48 cars
2. $1.50
3. 20 worms
4. 60 elastics
5. $28
6. 73 salamanders
7. $18.45
8. 3 cookies
9. 120 books
10. 27 juice boxes
11. 7 backpacks
12. $.16
13. 55 more minutes
14. 26,850 points
15. 8,600 points
16. $24.50

PAGE 58: Mix-a-Story

Answers will vary.

PAGE 59: Write Your Own!

Answers will vary.